T0157398

CUSTOMERS
Love 'Em or Lose 'Em

CUSTOMERS
Love 'Em or Lose 'Em

{ **57** ways to *love* your customers }

VINAY KUMAR

iUniverse, Inc.
Bloomington

Customers Love 'Em or Lose 'Em
57 Ways to Love Your Customers

iUniverse books may be ordered through booksellers or by contacting:

iUniverse
1663 Liberty Drive
Bloomington, IN 47403
www.iuniverse.com
1-800-Authors (1-800-288-4677)

ISBN: 978-1-4620-5658-3 (sc)
ISBN: 978-1-4620-5659-0 (e)

Printed in the United States of America

iUniverse rev. date: 09/26/2011

Dedication

This book is dedicated to everyone who makes the world a better place by giving their very best in service of others.

Table of Contents

Introduction

- Do you love your customers?
- Do they know it?
- Do they love you?

Simply put, if you don't love your customers, somebody else will, earning their business. Without customers, you have no business.

Some of the basic reasons businesses, big and small, lose customers include:

- Indifference
- Difficult to do business with
- Poor people skills
- Ineffective communication
- Inconsistency

Not only is losing customers costly, it costs much more to get new ones than to hold onto the ones you have. In addition, it's far easier to sell more to existing customers then to sell to new ones.

When your customers feel loved and cared for, they buy more, buy more often, are more loyal, are willing to pay more, and they actively refer you to their colleagues, friends and family. It also lowers your costs associated with business development. Furthermore, loving your customers truly makes business more enjoyable and all the hassles along with it more palatable.

Good news is that loving your customers and giving great service isn't rocket science. Rather it naturally emerges when you truly care about people, you choose to do your very best for others, and you have a strong inner desire to have a positive impact in the world.

With this in mind, I wrote this book to share with you 57 common sense ways you can love your customers, and in ways that are truly meaningful and memorable. These are based on my many years of firsthand experience in selling and servicing customers, both in retail and business to business.

Many of these I am sure you will already know. Key is to apply them. As you do, you will experience that such little actions taken on a consistent basis over time will lead to big results. And they will strengthen your customer relationships, your business, and make you more money.

So turn the pages for tips to show your love for those you serve for they are crucial to making your business the greater success it can be. To help you get the most from these tips, I have grouped them into chapters, as listed in the Table of Content.

I wish you the very best.

At Your Service,

Vinay Kumar

P.S. If you have any questions, please don't hesitate to reach out to me. I can be reached at vinay.vk.kumar@gmail.com.

Chapter 1

Know Your Customers

Tip No. 1
Different Strokes for Different Folks

Quality and Value - both very important, both hugely subjective and both determined in the customer's brain. And it's different for different customers.

Therefore, make time to get to know your customers. If you ask, they'll tell you how to sell to and service them. So asking questions and listening really pays off.

Ask them what's important to them, what matters to them, what they want, what makes them upset, how they want you to sell to and serve them, and so on. Ask, don't assume.

To help you start the dialogue, here are few simple questions to kick off the conversations:

- What are your goals, what are you trying to accomplish, and how does what we provide help you get what you want?
- What does great service to you look like and how do you know when you experience it?
- When it comes to working with us, what's important to you?
- On each of those areas, on a scale of 1-1o, how would you say we're doing?
- What specifically do you appreciate and value about our products and services, and why?
- What should we do better, differently, more of, less of, to better service you and deliver greater value? And how would that impact you?

- Is there anything else you would like to share that I haven't asked you about?

As for whom to ask, gather information from multiple touch points within each customer. Talk to everyone who is touched by your products and services. This includes for example those who make the purchases, receive your shipments, use your products, and pay your bills. Remember, every touch point leads to creating an overall customer experience.

As you learn what's important to them, get down to delivering what truly matters to your customers and what they value.

Tip No. 2
Listen with Intention

People often don't feel heard. Customers are people too. When you're with your customers (and prospects) put aside your cell phone and computers, your biases, your judgments, and your listening filters. Seek to first understand and appreciate their points of view.

Take time to truly listen to your customers, to both spoken and unspoken messages, needs and wants, challenges they're facing, what keeps them up at night, etc.

You will not only pick-up invaluable information that can help your business; it will also strengthen your relationships because you cared enough to truly listen. Real listening is a gift you give to another, and it doesn't cost you anything.

Tip No. 3
Help Make Dreams Come True

Beyond the term customer, they are human beings. Just like you and me, they have hopes and dreams.

Find out what matters most to them, what they want for themselves and their loved ones, what gives them joy, what they dream about.

Then to the extent you can, help them achieve those, even if it is only through your genuine encouragement.

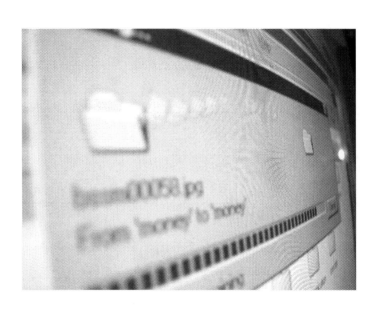

Tip No. 4
Share Information

Learn what your customers' interests are and what they are trying to achieve, personally and professionally. Then when you come across something that fits their interests and goals, send it to them along with a note reminding them the information made you think of them.

This can include items such as newspaper cuttings, articles and books. These things don't have to be expensive, or cost anything for that matter. What is more important is they are relevant and meaningful.

Tip No. 5
Take Genuine Interest

Be real. Be authentic. Routinely demonstrate genuine interest in your clients' success, their needs, and their wants. To the extent reasonable, put their interests ahead of your own.

If they succeed, then you are likely to be rewarded as well. As Zig Zigler, a highly successful sales professional, motivational speaker and trainer once said, help others get what they want, they'll help you get what you want.

Tip No. 6
Survey

Regularly survey your customers with written, or on-line, questionnaires. Also conduct focus groups and face-to-face and phone interviews.

When possible, use a neutral 3rd party so they can feel comfortable freely saying what is on their minds.

The feedback should be part of your ongoing self-evaluation. Once surveys are completed, share with them what you learned and what you will do with the findings.

You'll experience that just asking will help you improve customer retention for it shows you cared enough to ask.

Tip No. 7
Seek Advice

When making important decisions, especially ones that will impact your customers, ask for their input. They'll be happy you asked and will appreciate that you value their guidance.

In fact, consider forming a Customer Advisory Board. Invite your customers AND prospects to be on your advisory team, guiding you on how to best serve them, how to grow your business, and to share useful information with one another.

In my own experience, my customers have shown me not only how to best sell and service them; they have also kept me from making some costly mistakes. For there were times I thought something was a great idea but they felt otherwise. In the end, they are the customers so best to listen to them.

Chapter 2

Know Your Stuff

Tip No. 8
Be the Expert

In today's fast moving world, there is so much information that it's impossible for anyone to know everything and know it well. More than ever, customers want to work with people who are experts in their fields and know their businesses.

Therefore, know your products and services inside and out, know what you can do and what you can't. This will allow you to ask appropriate and relevant questions, as well as consistently provide correct information to your customer's questions.

In addition, customers often know what they want but don't always know how to express it clearly. Asking questions will help you help them crystallize their thoughts. With that clarity you will be in a far better position to deliver greatest value to them.

Tip No. 9
Teach

Freely share your knowledge and expertise, to help others succeed at what they do. Customers appreciate and value that you take an active interest in their success and are willing to share your expertise. This will help you become a highly valued resource and stand above others who provide similar products and services.

You will no longer be viewed as just another vendor. On the contrary, you will become the go-to-person, the expert who can help them solve their problems. You become the first-to-call, and price becomes far less of a factor in their decision to buy from you.

By doing so, you will also attract new customers. In my experience, teaching is one of the most effective ways of developing new business.

A special note on teaching here.

If you have facilities, often as possible, conduct sessions at your facilities. Bringing customers and prospects to your place will strengthen the connection and bond with your business and your team.

In addition, invite others who serve your customer base, but are not direct competitors, to also conduct educational workshops and seminars at your facilities. By doing so, they will invite their customers and prospects to your facilities and therefore you will be indirectly "marketing" your offerings to a broader audience, whom you might not reach otherwise.

This way you'll broaden your exposure and strengthen relationships with others who serve your customer base. Overtime they'll refer business to you and hopefully you'll also refer business to them.

It's a wonderful way to do business, to build community, in a way that's very meaningful, and where everyone wins.

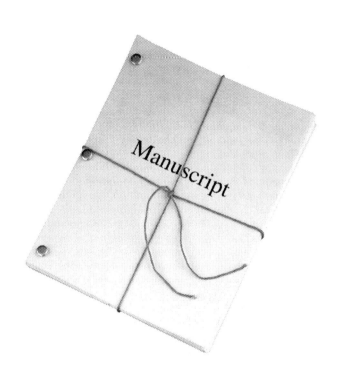

Tip No. 10
Write

Sharing information via articles, books, blogs, social marketing venues, electronic discussion groups, and correspondence will further increase your exposure and raise your reputation as a valuable resource.

As with teaching, writing will also help you not only strengthen your existing customer relationships, it will over time also lead to new customers. In my experience, writing is a great way to establish credibility, and increase exposure to yourself and your offerings.

In fact, in business-to-business settings, teaching combined with writing is one of the most effective ways of building your business.

Tip No. 11
Clarify

Customers know what they want but don't always know the best way to achieve it. Based on your expertise, help clarify what they really want to achieve and how to achieve it most effectively.

Offer ideas and solutions for consideration. If they like what they hear, they will commission your help further and see your value from new angles.

Chapter 3

Deliver

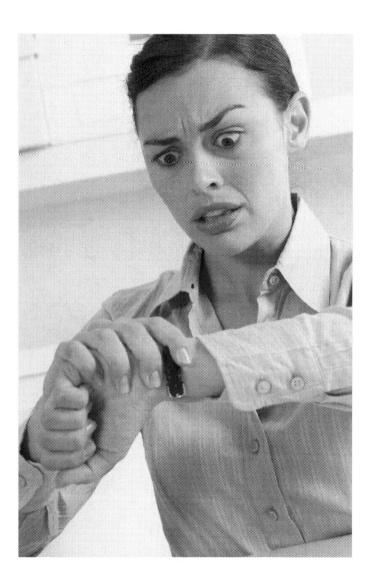

Tip No. 12
Get It Done, Done Right, On-Time, First-Time, Every Time

Clients are often on overload. There is too much to do in too little time. So the more you can do for them and the more you can make their life easier, the more valuable a resource you'll become.

Help them get their requirements met with minimal time required on their end. And after the project is completed be sure to follow-up and check in to make sure all went well. Very few do this. By doing so, you'll really stand out and will be remembered.

Tip No. 13
Communicate! Communicate!

Don't keep 'em guessing. No one likes to be in the dark. When customers don't know what's happening, they imagine the worst, causing them anxiety and worry. While this is human nature, you don't want to be the source of their worries. It won't serve you.

Keep your customers updated on your progress on their assignments and requests. Communicating regularly demonstrates your accountability, conveys your customer satisfaction emphasis, and that you're dedicated to serving them.

Along similar lines, if something isn't going quiet as planned, customers do understand, provided you inform with them within a reasonable time frame rather than surprising them with bad news at the last minute.

Therefore, when you do have to convey some "bad" news, at the same time, be sure to also let them know what you are doing to make it right, get it back on track. Your customers will appreciate it.

Finally, when in doubt, it's better to over communicate then under.

Tip No. 14
Save 'Em Money

Accept that everyone works hard for his or her money. Therefore if you see a way to help your customers save money, let them know. They'll come to recognize and value you as a business partner, and not merely a vendor.

This does not mean you should lower your prices. Making money is a good thing for it allows you to do even more for your people and for your customers. It simply means finding more effective and efficient ways to help your customers get what they want. In the end, it's more about delivering value then what you charge.

Tip No. 15
Be Honest

If you don't know something, admit it. Then go to work to find answers they're looking for and get back to your customers promptly. Strive to become a resource.

Clients don't expect you to know everything. But they do expect and appreciate your honesty and your willingness to go the extra mile to find the answers they are looking for.

Tip No. 16
Keep Your Promises

Do what you say you're going to do. When you make a promise, be sure to keep it. Your word is your bond and building your reputation for keeping your word and for being dependable is essential to earning the trust that will keep customers coming back to you again and again. It's a core principle for business success.

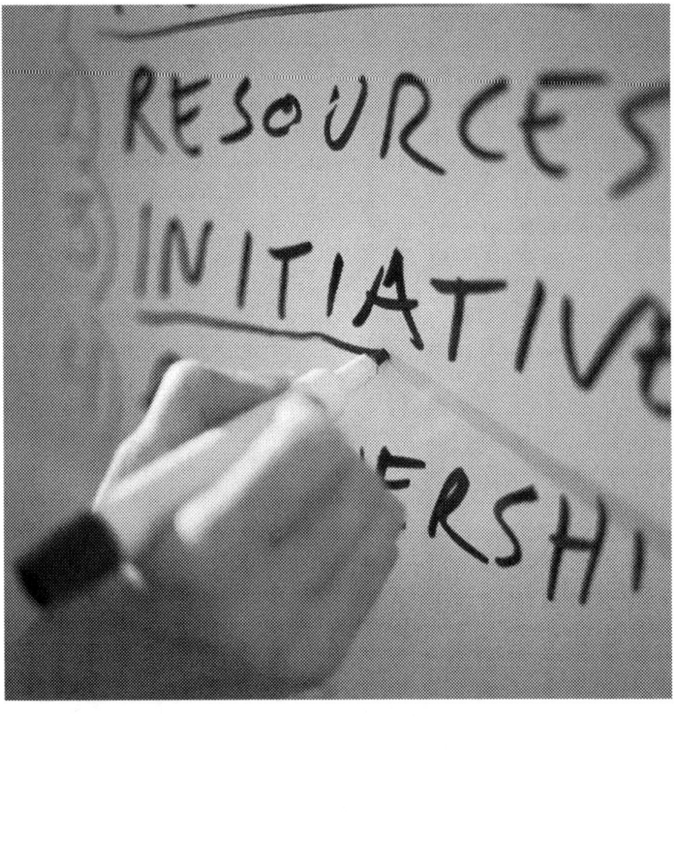
RESOURCES
INITIATIV

Tip No. 17
Anticipate

Be proactive. Take initiative. Anticipate what your customers will need, and offer solutions accordingly. For example if your customer orders French Fries, be sure to take ketchup with them. Don't wait for them to ask you for each and every little thing.

Tip No. 18
Be Predictable

Inconsistent service, the customer never knowing what he/ she will receive at any given point in time, drives customers crazy. When it comes to service, be dependable and predictably consistent in each and every interaction. It provides customers with a great peace of mind.

Similarly, whenever you make any customer impacting changes to your processes, be sure to let your customers know before those changes take effect. They will thank you for thinking of them and keeping them informed.

Tip No. 19
Make it Easy

Constantly be evaluating your policies, procedures and systems, and simplifying processes taking out anything that would aggravate customers. Keep ask questions such as:

- What can we do to make it easier for our customers to do business with us?
- What can we do to ensure each customer interaction is a pleasant experience for them, and for us?
- What choices can I make and actions I can take right now to provide more value, for both my people and my customers?

The easier and the more pleasant you are to work with and to do business with, the more business you will have.

Tip No. 20
Keep Score

I don't know about you but I find doing anything that I can't measure gets boring after sometime. Plus, my experience shows that what gets measured (and rewarded) gets done.

Therefore develop a scorecard, based on what's important to you and your customers. Then be sure to keep score and share relevant results with your entire team, as well as use the data to continuously improve your business and your products and services.

In addition, don't forget to celebrate your wins, as you make progress and hit those winning scores. It'll keep business enjoyable and interesting.

Tip No. 21
No One Does it Alone

From the Chief Executive Officer to the Chief Cleaning Officer, serving customers is everyone's job. No ifs and buts. It takes everyone working together to take care of customers. No position is more, or less, important than the other.

And frankly the customer doesn't care what your job title is and what you do. All they care is if you are solving their problems and fulfilling there needs and wants. If you're talking to the customer, regardless of your role and responsibilities, to them you are the company, and they expect you to take care of them.

Chapter 4

Make it Right

Tip No. 22
Let 'Em Vent

When a customer wants to vent, let 'em. Keep quiet and listen, with intention to understand. Do not interrupt or get defensive.

Many times their venting has little to do with you. After they finish letting off steam, calmly ask them what they want from you and what they want you to do to make it right. You'll find that most customers are fair and reasonable in their requests.

Customers understand that people make mistakes. While they don't expect you to be perfect, they do expect you to care when you screw up and to make it right.

Tip No. 23
Thank 'Em for Complaining

Work with any customer long enough, breakdown is bound to happen. See breakdowns as gifts because they point you to areas where you can do better.

Moreover, when something goes wrong, your response may be the only chance you'll get to show just how special you are. In my experience what separates service-focused companies from others is not that they are perfect but rather how they handle breakdowns when they do occur.

Therefore, when customers take the time to complain and offer you advice or feedback, accept it happily as a learning opportunity, regardless of whether or not it is actionable. Success often comes by associating with and being guided by others.

Tip No. 24
Make it Right

When something goes wrong, don't ignore the problem hoping it'll go away. Ignoring will only make matters worse. Instead, quickly take responsibility, apologize, and go to work to make it right.

The old movie said 'love means never having to say you're sorry". On the contrary, love means being able to say you're sorry, and know that the other party will be more understanding, as you are working to correct the matter.

In the long run, customers forget specifics of any given situation. But they always remember how you responded and how you took care of them (or didn't).

Tip No. 25
Don't Leave 'Em Hanging

If the customer makes a mistake with you, then too ask them what you can do to help remedy things. To err is human! Show them that you recognize that we all make mistakes and take the long view even it may require some expense at your end. They will be more likely to reciprocate when the roles are reversed.

.

Think of each customer in-terms of life-time-value, the amount of profitable business you can reasonably expect from them over time. So if this means at times you have to give a little, that's OK. Remember, you want to win the war, even if it means occasionally losing a battle.

Tip No. 26
Take the High Road

Don't play the blame game. No one likes it and no one wins in such a game. Instead, focus on finding win-win solutions, making things right, no matter who is at fault.

Customers tend to forget who was at fault and what happened even. But they do remember how you handled the situation. In other words while they tend to forget the specifics they do remember the feelings. Better to leave off with good impressions and good feelings.

Tip No. 27
Take Ownership

When a customer has a request or a complaint, don't pass it on to someone else. When you take the call, own it, 'till the customer is satisfied.

As an added note, when you receive any complaint, in addition to resolving that particular issue to your client's complete satisfaction, use this as an additional opportunity to review your system and processes to determine the root of what might have led to the complaint. Then go to work to improve your system so it does not repeat.

Think in-terms of continuous improvement. Constantly review your entire process, from initial customer contact to delivery to billing. Look for opportunities to make improvements to each and every touch point and for ways of doing business with you to be as easy and as pleasant as possible. Strive for perfection.

Chapter 5

Build Strong Relationships

Tip No. 28
Impressions

Appearances matter, for perceptions are reality.

Smile. Dress professionally. Practice personal hygiene. Keep your equipment and surroundings areas clean and organized. Package your products professionally and neatly. Look nice. Smell nice. Talk in friendly tone. Create positive impressions in each and every interaction.

When all is said and done, people do business with people they like. So be nice to do business with.

$$E_2 = IR_2 = 0.5 \times 10 = 5 \text{ volts}$$

$$E_3 = IR_3 = 0.5 \times 50 = 25 \text{ volts}$$

$$E_4 = IR_4 = 0.5 \times 30 = 15 \text{ volts}$$

$$E_T = E_1 + E_2 + E_3 + E_4$$

$$E_T = 5 + 5 + 25 + 15 = 50 \text{ volts}$$

(c) Power consumed in R_1 is:

$$P_1 = IE_1 = 0.5 \times 5 = 2.5 \text{ watts}$$

$$P_2 = IE_2 = 0.5 \times 5 = 2.5 \text{ watts}$$

Tip No. 29
Be Mindful of Language, Please

Speak your customers' language. Minimize use of acronyms and jargon that are specific to your business and which your customers may not fully understand.

Many will not ask you to explain what you are really saying. Feeling uncomfortable some will instead choose to take their business elsewhere. Don't make your customers feel stupid and uncomfortable.

Speaking of language, it's important to note when working cross-culturally, gestures and words have different connotations in different places. So be extra sensitive to your body language, gestures and word choices.

Tip No. 30
Take Care of Your People

Critical to loving your customers is loving your people. Your people are your point of delivery, where "rubber meets the road". Highly motivated enthusiastic team members are more likely to work hard to take good care of your customers.

Opposite is also true. When your people aren't happy and they feel as if you don't care about them, it's highly unlikely they'll work hard to make your customers happy.

As I always say, take care of your people and they'll take care of you and your customers.

Tip No. 31
Take Care of Yourself

If you're not happy, you'll find it difficult to make others happy. So first be true to yourself and be happy. Accept yourself as you are for you are perfect just as you are.

Take time to understand how you are being, and what you are being and doing when you are at your best for that will point you to your inherent gifts/talents. Then leverage your unique gifts in service of others.

By doing so, you'll experience greater joy and will make a greater positive difference in the lives of others.

Tip No. 32
Get Along

One of the biggest reasons people don't get along is simply due to lack of understanding. Take time to understand yourself and understand others.

By focusing more on what makes each individual special and what value they add, you will develop a greater appreciation for yourself and for others. In the process will come to better get along with others.

This is crucial for extraordinary relationships provide the foundation upon which extraordinary results are achieved.

Tip No. 33
Be Active in Groups

Belong to and actively participate in groups where your customers belong. By doing so, you will make many more contacts that will lead to further strengthening your existing relationships, develop new ones, which in turn will help your business grow further. This will also help you better understand their desires and challenges by closely interacting with them on their turf.

In addition, be sure to seek out opportunities to write, speak, and teach to share your knowledge and expertise. Not only will your existing customers appreciate it, you will further establish credibility and increase exposure, which over time will lead to new customers too.

Thank You ありがとう。TACK

grazie Bedankt Danke Schön merci

MERCI OBRIGADO gracias GRAZIE GRACIAS

Tack Merci bedankt THANK YOU

DANKE SCHÖN obrigado

Gracias Bedankt Obrigado

thank you danke schön

תודה BEDANKT Merci

ありがとう。 tack TACK

Gracias THANK YOU gracias Grazie

Danke Schön شكراً bedankt

OBRIGADO merci תודה

MERCI thank you grazie

obrigado gracias Merci GRAZIE

merci gracias Thank You

tack תודה bedankt Bedankt شكراً

BEDANKT grazie

תודה THANK YOU Danke Schön

Tip No. 34
Say Thank You

Two simple words, yet they mean so much.

Speaking of Thank You, when was the last time someone sent you a hand written thank you note? Or you sent one to your customers? They are so rare these days that when your customers receive one, it really stands out and is remembered.

Btw, thank you for reading my book.

Tip No. 35
Be Accessible

Be available when they need you. If you cannot deal with someone immediately at least acknowledge him or her immediately. People do not mind waiting. What frustrates them is feeling ignored.

Also, if you're heading out on vacation, to a conference, a training program and you know you won't be accessible, let the customers know in advance, along with information on who they can contact in your absence. It aggravates customers immensely when they need you and you're nowhere to be found.

Speaking of being accessible, choose people over technology, as much as possible. It's aggravating to be caught-up in endless options built into automated phone systems, for example. Make it easy for your customers to speak with real people.

Tip No. 36
Do Coffee

Lunches can get expensive. Meetings over coffee are more reasonable and often more conducive to richer deeper more relaxed conversations, that are not interrupted by waiters and chewing food.

Meeting over coffee also gets your clients out of the office, in the morning typically, and does not leave them with the feeling that the day is rapidly evaporating with late afternoon returns to work.

Tip No. 37
Respect

Treat others, as they want to be treated. It is the Platinum Rule in all aspects of life. Respect your clients, their decisions, and their choices.

Show respect also by returning calls promptly, letting them know when you'll be away, truly listening, and addressing their needs and concerns in a timely manner. Such small actions impact relationships in a big way. Btw, speaking of returning calls, you may be surprised to know how many people don't return calls at all. Just returning calls alone will set you apart.

Finally, remember that respect, like love, has to be given away before it can be received. Few customers will ever respect you until you respect them first.

Tip No. 38
Connect

Introduce your customers to others in your network whom you believe they'll benefit by knowing. Provide leads. Help them generate opportunities. Promote your customers' products and services as well use 'em yourself whenever possible.

Typically, both parties will appreciate your thinking of them and they will refer others to you and help you to expand your business circle too.

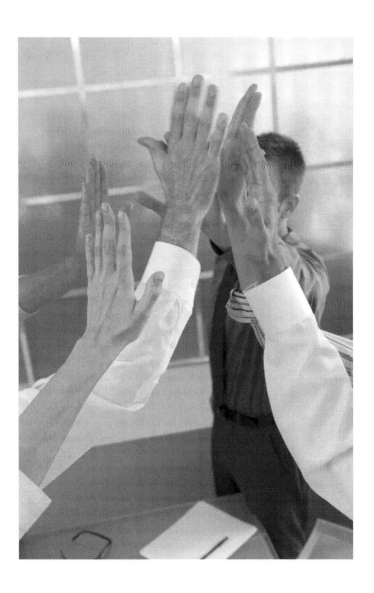

Tip No. 39
Celebrate

Celebrate your customer' successes, even when they have nothing to do with your business. For example, when they get a promotion or the company wins a contract or grant. Express your happiness and invite them to a celebratory lunch or drink and toast their continuing success.

Tip No. 40
Be Kind

From time to time, we all face difficult times in our lives. Stand by and with those who are facing difficult challenges. From a place of genuine caring, offer your assistance as best as you can.

You never know what someone is going through, so be kind, be gentle and be patient in your dealings. Remember what goes around truly does come around when you are faced with your own challenges.

Tip No. 41
Be a Sounding Board

Often it helps to have a third-party to talk to, with whom you can bounce ideas off of and who will offer an outside voice to help sort through issues being faced. Offer to be such a person to your customers and make the time to do so.

Tip No. 42
Personalize Your Communications

Your customers are real people. Call them by their names. Let them know you know them, and invite them to call you by your first name as well. It is not a sign of informality, but rather familiarity.

A special note here in regards to your being formal or informal when addressing your customers and prospects. Different cultures have different "rules of engagement".

In some cultures how you address someone depends on for example their position, gender and age. When in doubt, ask how they would like to be addressed. They will respect you for being sensitive and respectful.

Tip No. 43
Refer 'Em to Your Competitors

When you feel a competitor will be able to do a better job for your customer, you should then refer them there. At a minimum, mention the option to your client.

They'll respect you for it and it will contribute to building trust, which is so important to lasting meaningful relationships of all kinds. As an added bonus, you may just turn your competitor into a friend also and they may in turn refer business to you.

Everyone wins.

Tip No. 44
Acknowledge

Take the customer seriously. He is always right, especially when he's wrong! He is right about how he feels and he is right in that he can leave your business and tell the world that you and your company stinks. So - take the customer very seriously!

When in doubt, remember these two rules when working with customers:

Rule No. 1: The customer is always right
Rule No. 2: If the customer is wrong, see rule no. 1

Tip No. 45
Help 'Em Find Work

If and when needed and you can, tap into your network, helping your customers find work opportunities.

Send them job announcements, request for proposals, and words of encouragement. They will appreciate your friendship at their time of need.

Tip No. 46
Send Thanksgiving Cards

Many send year-end cards, a time when your greetings can get lost in the clutter. Instead, send cards at Thanksgiving. Then go further and personalize them. Include a handwritten note even.

Say something like: "Thank you so much Jim, for your business. We really appreciate it. – Suzie"

Good business includes re-affirming relationships and expressing your thanks.

Tip No. 47
Hold an Open House

Invite customers to visit your facilities, meet the team, to get to know your organization and the people who deliver their goods and services.

Open houses can strongly contribute to lasting impressions. But of course you must have your house in order if the takeaway is to be a positive one.

Tip No. 48
Keep in Touch

Even when a customer leaves his/her current employment, stay in touch. Think long-term because a change of venue does not necessarily equate with you'll no longer doing business with them.

They will keep you in their thoughts for referrals and perhaps one day again become your customer. Remember the old adage, "Out of sight, out of mind!"

Speaking of keeping in touch make sure you are easily accessible to your customers. Make it easy for them to find you when they need you. Don't make them run around looking for you. And when they need you, be sure to respond in a timely manner.

Tip No. 49
Do Something for the Kids

When you're giving out stuff, give something they'll pass on to their children. When they see their kids happily play with your stuff, they'll experience both joy, and they'll silently thank you.

A client I recall adopted a daughter from overseas, who was having trouble learning English. As my daughter had similar challenges, I sent her set of audiotapes that helped my daughter overcome similar difficulties. Twenty years later, whenever I meet this person, she still remembers that kindness and thanks profusely.

So find out what's happening in your customers' lives, beyond just work. Then support them in every way you can, as much as you can.

Tip No. 50
Give Your Best to Your Best

While all human beings are created equal, when it comes to customers, some are more equal than others.

When you analyze source of your revenue and profits, you'll come to see that it's often a small percentage of your customers who give you the greatest share of your revenue and your profits.

Be sure to identify who they are and give them your very best service. Furthermore, identify common characteristics of your best customers and then work to find more new customers just like them.

As you do this, you'll make much greater gains for your given efforts and investments.

Tip No. 51
Have a Cookout

Invite your clients and prospects to a barbeque. Make it a day of fun and games. Ask them to bring families too. You will be creating community.

Of course, of those you are inviting, be mindful of their dietary preferences and be sensitive to religious and cultural restrictions.

When in doubt, ask your guests ahead of time their preferences. They will gladly share with you what they prefer and what they do and don't eat and drink.

Tip No. 52
Take a Hike

Pull a group together and go for hikes. Make it a fun and a special day. Bring sandwiches and drinks, enjoy the day and get some exercise together.

When people enjoy being together, that often leads to greater affinity and better communication, which ultimately contributes to results.

Tip No. 53
Spread Joy

Surprise 'em with movie tickets and snack gift certificates, or tickets to other events that your customers would enjoy. It reminds people of work-life balance and they won't forget who contributed to theirs.

Tip No. 54
Cook Together

Some of my customers loved to learn how to cook Indian food. So from to time, I would have cooking sessions at my home where we cooked favorite dishes together. It made for very memorable and fun evenings and the guests reciprocated with pleasure.

Tip No. 55
Put Your Hobbies to Work

Do you or a family member like to bake or make your own jars of jam? If so, baked goods and jams make great gifts to customers.

Send them a batch of your best cookies, a jar of jam, a loaf of bread or one of your pies or cakes. Homemade makes it even more a special gift to the recipient.

It's a special touch. Share these in particular with your best customers and watch those relationships become even stronger.

Tip No. 56
Fire Customers from Hell

This is something I don't recommend you do lightly. Rather it's a measure of very last resort.

If a customer is truly impossible to please despite your numerous efforts, divorce yourself from the relationship. They suck up too much of your time and energy, keeping you from giving your best to your best customers. Plus it's always more fun and productive to work with clients you love and who love you and appreciate you. You both deserve it.

Of course, part ways in a friendly and respectful manner. Just because it didn't work out doesn't make them bad people. It just wasn't meant to work out with you, in-terms of business, at this point in time. Moreover, times change, situations change, people change. So who knows, maybe one day you'll do business together again and that time it'll work.

Tip No. 57
Never Stop Learning

Continue to expand your knowledge on how to love your customers. Here are some of my favorite books on the topic:

☐ Raving Fans by Ken Blanchard
☐ Moments of Truth by Jan Carlzon
☐ Up Your Service by Ron Kaufman
☐ Customers for Life by Carl Sewell

In addition, engage your customers in conversations on an on-going basis. To get invaluable insights, nothing beats the power of such conversations. Ask them open-ended questions such as what makes them happy and what annoys them. You'll gain invaluable insights that when applied, will help you be even more successful.

Conclusion

Business success in my experience comes from sum of small steps, taken repeatedly, on a consistent basis. And when it comes to service, it's the little things, often thing that often barely cost any money, that lead to big results. In this book, you learned about many such "little things".

Apply these 57 tips, as they best fit your situation, to show your love for your customers. By doing so, you will cultivate customer loyalty and improve your life, outlook and business success. Guaranteed!

About the Author

Vinay Kumar is passionate about service and leveraging that to drive loyalty, profits and revenue growth.

He serves as the Director of Customer Support at TEOCO Corporation, a US based firm with offices in US, India, Europe, Israel and Costa Rica. TEOCO develops mission critical software solutions for the telecom sector, and has clients around the globe.

Prior to joining TEOCO, he co-owned a successful family business where he was responsible for B2B sales, marketing and customer service. He was instrumental in achieving exponential growth, much of which he attributes to applying these 57 tips he shares in this book.

His in-depth experience also includes Fortune 100, Federal Government, non-profits, associations, consulting, and manufacturing. Roles he has held range from leading to selling to serving customers, for small and large organizations.

He has authored articles and publications on the topics of planning, business development, sales, customer service and communication. He has been nationally recognized by the American Society of Association Executives (ASAE) for providing outstanding service to the association community.

Vinay can be reached at:

E: KumarV@teoco.com
E: Vinay.VK.Kumar@gmail.com
B: VinayKumarCoach.BlogSpot.com
P: 703-851-9466